THE BEST OF
GAMING

SUPERSTARS OF GAMING

Laura Hamilton Waxman

Lerner Publications ◆ Minneapolis

Lerner Publications Company
An imprint of Lerner Publishing Group, Inc.
241 First Avenue North
Minneapolis, MN 55401 USA

For reading levels and more information, look up this title at www.lernerbooks.com.

Main body text set in ITC Franklin Gothic Std.
Typeface provided by Adobe Systems.

Editor: Alison Lorenz **Designer:** Viet Chu

Library of Congress Cataloging-in-Publication Data

Names: Waxman, Laura Hamilton, author.
Title: Superstars of gaming / Laura Hamilton Waxman.
Description: Minneapolis : Lerner Publications, 2021 | Series: The best of gaming (UpDog Books) | Includes bibliographical references and index. | Audience: Ages 8–13 | Audience: Grades K–1 | Summary: "The biggest stars of gaming draw in millions of dollars and fans. Meet the greatest streamers, creators, and players in this look at the top of the gaming world."— Provided by publisher.
Identifiers: LCCN 2019043126 (print) | LCCN 2019043127 (ebook) | ISBN 9781541590502 (library binding) | ISBN 9781728401195 (ebook)
Subjects: LCSH: Video gamers—Juvenile literature. | Video games—Juvenile literature.
Classification: LCC GV1469.3 .W468 2021 (print) | LCC GV1469.3 (ebook) | DDC 794.8—dc23

LC record available at https://lccn.loc.gov/2019043126
LC ebook record available at https://lccn.loc.gov/2019043127

Manufactured in the United States of America
1-47569-48099-1/24/2020

Table of Contents

Gaming Fame

Imagine crushing the competition while two million fans watch.

Kyle "Bugha" Giersdorf did just that. The American teen won $3 million in the first *Fortnite* World Cup.

Superstars such as Giersdorf
wow fans with their skills.

Gamers and creators work hard to make it to the top.

creators: people who make video games

UP NEXT!
A LOOK AT THE
BIGGEST GAMERS.

Superstar Gamers

Lee "Faker" Sang-hyeok is one of the best *League of Legends* players.

He led his pro team to
three world championships.

pro: done as a job to make money

Sasha "Scarlett" Hostyn was the first woman to win a big *StarCraft II* tournament.

She's the top-earning
woman gamer in the world.

top-earning: winning the most prize
money as a competitor

BIO BREAK!

Name: Ksenia "vilga" Klyuenkova
Age: 28
Hometown: Moscow, Russia
Claim to fame: top-earning female *CS: GO* player

Name: Katherine "Mystik" Gunn
Age: 31
Hometown: Palmdale, California
Claim to fame: top-earning female *Halo: Reach* player

Name: Peter "ppd" Dager
Age: 27
Hometown: Fort Wayne, Indiana
Claim to fame: one of the top-earning *Dota 2* players

Name: Tyler "Ninja" Blevins

Age: 28

Hometown: Grayslake, Illinois

Claim to fame: most popular streamer

Name: Stephanie "FemSteph"

Age: 31

Home country: USA

Claim to fame: earns thousands playing *Fortnite*

Name: Magnus Carlsen

Age: 28

Hometown: Tonsberg, Norway

Claim to fame: chess world champion

streamer: a gamer who posts live videos online

Marcelo "coldzera" David is one of the world's best CS: GO players.

He leads his teams to victory year after year.

UP NEXT!
MEET THE CREATORS BEHIND YOUR FAVORITE GAMES.

Superstar Creators

Game maker Satoshi Tajiri loved collecting bugs as a kid.

He used that love to design
Nintendo's Pokémon series.

design: to create a new
idea for a game and figure
out how it will be played

series: a set of games
that are part of the same
story or world

Gamer Tips: *Pokémon Go*

➤ If you walk away or wait at the start of the game, Pikachu will spawn.

➤ You can skip the egg hatch animation. Pinch your screen instead of tapping it.

➤ Use a Lucky Egg to get more XP.

➤ Manage your bag. Keep only the Pokémon that will help you in Gym and Raid battles.

Jane McGonigal studied game design. She also studied what makes people happy.

She created *SuperBetter* to help
people feel better about themselves.

These superstar gamers and creators have taken the gaming world by storm.

Glossary

creators: people who make video games

design: to create a new idea for a game and figure out how it will be played

pro: done as a job to make money

series: a set of games that are part of the same story or world

streamer: a gamer who posts live videos online

top-earning: winning the most prize money as a competitor

Check It Out!

Carmichael, L. E. *How Do Video Games Work?* Minneapolis: Lerner Publications, 2016.
Learn how video games work and about the parts inside a game console.

Guinness World Records. *Guinness World Records 2020: Gamer's Edition.* London: Guinness World Records, 2020.
Meet gaming's world record holders.

Jane McGonigal's Official Website
https://janemcgonigal.com/
Learn about McGonigal and the games she's created.

Kyle "Bugha" Giersdorf's Official Website
https://bugha.net/
Find out more about the *Fortnite* champion.

The Official Pokémon Website
https://www.pokemon.com/us/
This website is your one-stop shop for everything Pokémon.

Scholastic. *Game On! 2020.* New York: Scholastic, 2020.
Read all about the latest and greatest games.

Index

Photo Acknowledgments

Image credits: picture alliance/Getty Images, p. 4; JOHANNES EISELE/AFP/Getty Images, p. 5; Mike Stobe/Getty Images, p. 6; The Asahi Shimbun/Getty Images, p. 7; Christoph Soeder/picture alliance/Getty Images, pp. 8, 9; Joe Scarnici/Getty Images, p. 10; ©ESL Gaming, p. 11; Gonzalo Arroyo Moreno/Getty Images, p. 12; Nicky J Sims/Kaspersky Lab/Getty Images, p. 13; Cooper Neill/ Getty Images, p. 14; Derry Ainsworth/Getty Images, p. 15; Stephen Lovekin/Getty Images, p. 16; Joe Scarnici/Nintendo of America/Getty Images, p. 17; Mindy Best/WireImage/Getty Images, pp. 19, 20; Lars Baron/Riot Games Inc./Getty Images, p. 21.

Design elements: Nusha777/iStock/Getty Images; cundra/iStock/ Getty Images.

Cover image: Eric Ananmalay/ESPAT Media/Getty Images.